THIS JOURNAL BELONGS TO:

Made in the USA
Las Vegas, NV
30 June 2024

91718602R00083